HANDSPINNER'S HANDBOOK

Library of Congress Catalog Card No. 76-12949
ISBN 0-9600990-1-8

Publisher: Bette Hochberg
333 Wilkes Circle, Santa Cruz, Ca. 95060

Wholesale Distributor: Straw Into Gold
P.O. Box 2904, Oakland, Ca. 94618

One day a friend opened a bag and spilled out shining silk. I watched it fall like a cascade of molten gold. I had spun wool before, but that silk opened the door that let in camels, goats, rabbits, alpacas, and many more.

We are the first handspinners in history to have access to animal and vegetable fibres from all over the world. I have included twenty fibres that are readily available. I have personally tested and spun these fibres many times, so I can be sure of what I write.

Through the ages, handspinning has been a practical necessity. Fast and simple ways of doing things were essential. Today, many unnecessarily slow, complex and esoteric methods are being used. This book gives simple directions for handling all fibres, and for becoming a fast, competent spinner.

Thank you, Susan Druding, for spilling out that silk. And thank you, Bernie Hochberg, for helping me with this book.

Bette Hochberg

CONTENTS

WHAT SPINNING IS . . .

You can spin almost anything that is long, thin and flexible–the hair of many animals and the fibres of many plants. It's even possible to sit in the woods and spin dry grasses without any tools. This is fun. But while learning, stay with the fibres that people have spun for centuries.

Spinning is holding a mass of fibres, and twisting a few of them as they are pulled from the loose mass. The rhythm is–"first twist, then pull".

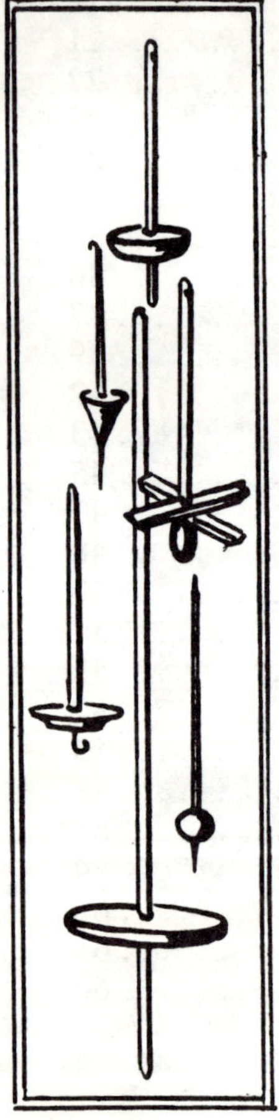

People have been spinning for at least 7,000 years. The earliest archeological finds of yarns were in the valley of the Nile. These were linen-like fibres. Early Egyptian wall paintings show the preparation and spinning of flax. About 6,000 years ago in Babylonia and Mesopotamia, sheep were domesticated and wool was spun and traded. For 5,000 years cotton has been grown and spun. China began its silk industry about 2,500 B.C. These four fibres–linen, cotton, wool, silk–supplied most of man's needs through the ages.

The handspindle. The first form of spinning was twisting by hand, or "thigh spinning". This is still done today by the Chilkat Indians. Then spinners discovered the handspindle: a stick with a weight which spins like a top. As the spindle revolves, the yarn twists, and is then wound around the shaft. During the 7,000 years that we have known how to spin, almost 6,500 of those years were spent with only the handspindle.

There are many sizes and styles of handspindles: little needle-like slivers of bamboo weighted with tiny beads of clay, and the long-shafted Navajo spindle with plate-like wooden whorls. It is possible to spin a finer thread on a handspindle than on a wheel. The Dacca muslins of India are woven of spindle-spun cotton so fine it measures 250 miles to a pound. Many cultures around the world still use handspindles.

The spinning wheel. The spinning wheel evolved from the handspindle. The earliest wheels were simply a long-shafted handspindle with the whorl suspended horizontally between two vertical posts. A cord encircled the spindle whorl and a larger wheel. Each time the large wheel revolved one turn, the little whorl revolved many turns. The spinner turned the large wheel with one hand and spun the yarn with the other hand—and wound it on the spindle shaft. This style was used for centuries in the Orient and was introduced to the West about 1400.

By 1480 the flyer was in use. The flyer holds a bobbin on its center shaft. The two revolve at different speeds and thus the yarn winds on as it is spun. Legend attributes the invention of the flyer to Leonardo da Vinci and its first production to Herr Jurgen of Brunswick Germany in 1533. However, the woodcut on this page, taken from the "Hausbuch" of the Waldburg family dated 1480, clearly shows a flyer in use. Two empty bobbins are lying on the bottom shelf. This is an earlier date than other books have assigned to the flyer, but the woodcut shows this is correct.

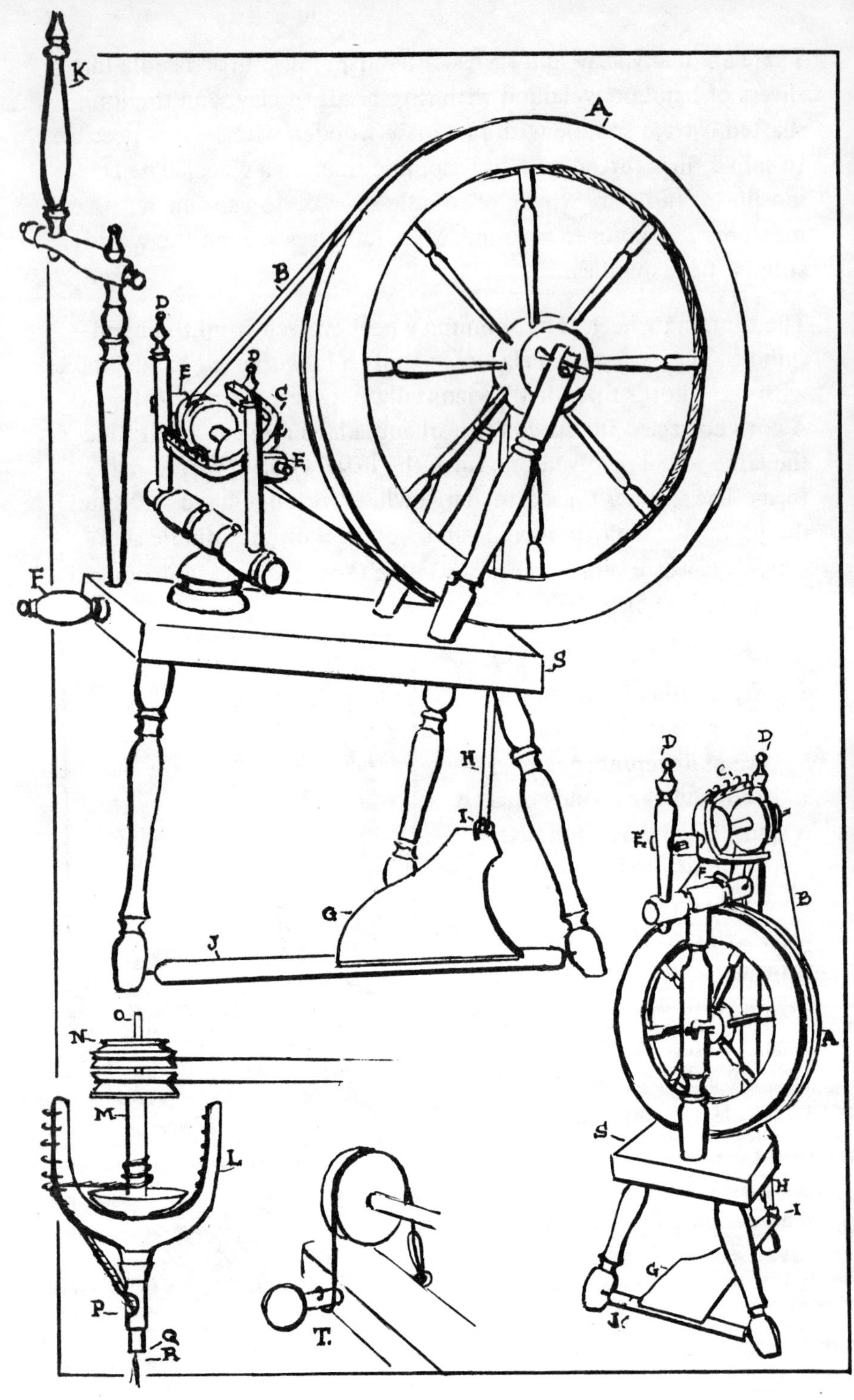
K
A
B
D
E
D
C
E
F
S
H
I
G
J
D
D
C
E
F
B
A
S
H
I
G
J
O
N
M
L
P
Q
R
T.

PARTS OF THE SPINNING WHEEL

A. **Wheel.**
B. **Drive band**–strong flexible cord.
C. **Flyer assembly**–holds bobbin and whorl.
D. **Maidens**–uprights at each end of flyer.
E. **Bearings**–on maidens; hold flyer assembly.
F. **Tension screw**–adjusts the yarn twist and rate of wind-on.
G. **Treadle**–rotates large wheel.
H. **Footman**–crank attaches it to axle of large wheel.
I. **Treadle cord**–attaches footman to treadle with a snug tie.
J. **Treadle bar**–metal pins on each end hold it to front legs.
K. **Distaff**–wooden arm to which unspun fibres can be tied or wrapped.
L. **Flyer**–metal shaft runs through center. Guide hooks on side.
M. **Bobbin**–turns freely on flyer shaft. Spun yarn winds around it.
N. **Whorl**–wooden disc screws onto metal shaft of the flyer. If it has two grooves, you can spin at two speeds.
O. **Shaft**–holds the bobbin and whorl within the flyer.
P. **Eye**–opening on top of metal shaft.
Q. **Orifice**–diameter determines maximum thickness of yarn that can be spun.
R. **Starter cord**–two feet long, tied around bobbin and not removed when you skein off yarn.
S. **Table.**
T. **Scotch tension**–some wheels like the Ashford have a single drive band going around the large wheel and whorl. A thin cord attaches to a spring or elastic on one side–goes over the bobbin groove–and winds onto a wooden peg on the other side. Turning this peg adjusts the yarn twist and rate of wind-on.

NOTE: Some wheels have a single drive band with a bobbin lead. A screw in the bearing on the front maiden adjusts the tension. When the bearing is tightened the tension increases.

Many new styles of wheels are being made in the U.S. but, to date, the principles and operation remain the same.

Advantages of the "long draw" method of spinning. The best way to evaluate information about how to spin is to ask yourself, "Could my ancestors have used this method and spun enough for their clothing and household use?" One often sees spinners hovering over the orifice of the wheel and working equally with their two hands–pulling out fibres with one hand and drawing back with the other. I call this the "push-pull" method. This is an easy way to teach beginners to spin, but you cannot become a good, fast and uniform spinner using this method. Your left hand *cannot* consistently pull out the same amount of fibre, and it is necessarily a slow process that cannot be speeded up. Hobby spinners and craft books have been perpetuating this awkward and inefficient technique.

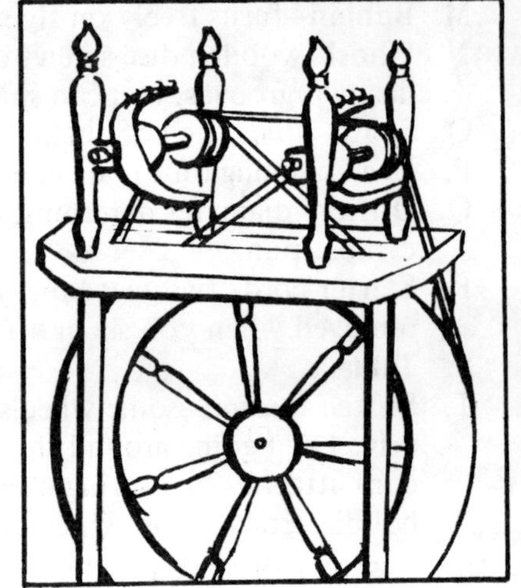

In past centuries all spinning was done with the "long draw" of one hand. Supported handspindles and hand-turned wheels left only one hand free for spinning. Wheels with two flyers, such as the one shown here, were intended to be used by one spinner. A pamphlet published in London in 1681 shows this wheel and states its purpose is to double the production of one spinner using flax or wool. It was only when the need for hand spinning declined that it began to be called a "gossip wheel" and "lovers wheel".

Once you become adept at the "long draw", you will be treadling as rapidly as is comfortable, and drawing your arm back in a long sweep. Your arm will move back, keeping just enough ahead of the twist to allow free drawing out of the fibres in your right hand. It is smooth, rhythmic and rapid. This is the only feasible way to spin short-staple fibres such as cotton, cashmere, camel down. I spin all fibres this way–except line and extra-thick yarn. I can spin a pound an hour of wool, linen or mohair on a saxony wheel.

Wheels drink lots of oil. It is not possible to give a wheel too much oil. Very few spinners give enough oil to their wheels. While I am spinning, I oil my wheel every few hours. It takes only a minute and it will speed up your spinning and make it easier.

There are always conflicting rumors handed about on what should and should not be used to lubricate the leather on wheels. It is true that all leather will eventually rot. If you have a modern wheel, the leather will probably have a life-span equal to your own, whatever lubricant you use. So oil all moveable parts with a light-weight oil, like 3-in-1 oil (or mineral oil). You can hold a paper towel to catch the excess under the part you are oiling – but saturate it.

Start with the treadle. Drop oil into the holes where metal pins hold the treadle bar to the front legs. Oil the treadle cord. If the center axle is not sealed with bearings, oil the axle and the groove that the axle turns in. Oil the top of the footman. Remove the flyer assembly. Oil the bearings on the front and back maidens. Remove the whorl and bobbin from the flyer and oil the center metal shaft of the flyer. Drip a drop of oil down the center of each bobbin, and reassemble.

Now treadle, and the wheel should turn very freely with just a light touch of your foot to the treadle. If you rapidly treadle a wheel that is in top condition, and remove your foot from the treadle, it should continue to revolve as many as 20 times.

If you have any wooden screws on your wheel, grease them about every six months. Many wheels have wooden tension screws and some, like the Finnish wheel, have wood screws to hold the wheel axle in place. Wood that is not greased tends to lock together. Use bar soap or any kind of thick grease, like the kind for cars, or even vegetable shortening. Early spinners used sheep fat.

Drive band. The drive band is the string which goes around the large wheel and makes the spindle whorl turn. The best drive band

I have found is a 10 or 12-ply cotton parcel post twine. Even tightly-spun wool will stretch. Linen is strong but becomes slippery after a few hours and can no longer "grab" the wheel. Cotton wears well and is sensitive to the wheel. Good spinners usually advise overlapping the ends and sewing to splice. However, when I'm in a hurry I make a small square knot or weaver's knot, and closely clip the ends. A heavy knot on a thick drive band is hard on the wheel and breaks the rhythm of your spinning. You should not be able to feel the knot while you spin.

When you tie the drive band on, first loosen the screw which moves the flyer assembly close to the big wheel, so it will be easier to tie it on snugly. Tie it considerably less taut than a guitar string. Never put a smooth finish on the wheel groove. If it is already smooth, rough it up with coarse sandpaper.

A good place to sit. Your wheel should sit on the hard bare floor. (If you have carpeting, it will help to put a square of plywood under the wheel.) If your wheel is on a spongy surface, this puts a strain on the structure of the wheel, and makes treadling more difficult.

Don't slouch on a couch or soft arm chair. Find a stable backless stool. Try a kitchen stool, a piano stool, or even a small barrel. Stand beside the stool barefoot. If the top of the stool is even with the botton of your kneecap, it is about the right height. It will likely be between 17 and 18 inches. Sit close to the wheel and to the left of center. With good posture you will tire less quickly.

When you are spinning wool "in the grease", it's nice to sit in the sun or by the fire. The heat warms the lanolin and the fibres will draw out more easily. Never leave your wheel sitting in a hot place any longer than necessary. If you leave your wheel sitting by a sunny window, the heat will dry out the wood and sometimes crack it. If the wood has an oil finish, re-oil it regularly.

Treadling. If you are a beginner, your feet will work much faster than your hands. Without spinning, practice treadling as slowly as possible and still keep the wheel turning clockwise. Practice stopping and starting up again in a clockwise direction. This is important because beginning spinners often forget and allow the wheel to reverse its direction. Try to think of other things, or read a book while you do this. Your foot should learn to treadle automatically without any directions from your head.

When you begin spinning you will find that the speed of treadling will affect the amount of twist in your yarn. The faster you treadle, the more it will twist. A bare foot is more sensitive to the treadle than a shoe.

Starting cord and threading hook. Take a piece of string about two feet long—a fuzzy, hairy wool yarn works best. Tie one end firmly around the center core of the bobbin and wind it around three or four times. Now you will need a threading hook. If your wheel doesn't have one, a crochet hook will work, or a bent paper clip. (I took a three-inch length of fancy turned dowel and inserted half a large paper clip into one end.) Take the end of your starting cord and pass it around the hooks on one side of your flyer, and hold it with your left hand over the eye on top of the spindle shaft. With the threading hook in your right hand, reach it into the orifice, and use it to bring the end of the starting cord down through the eye and out of the orifice. It sometimes helps beginners to tie a small knot an inch or two from the end of the starting cord—this makes it easier for the spinning fibre to catch onto it.

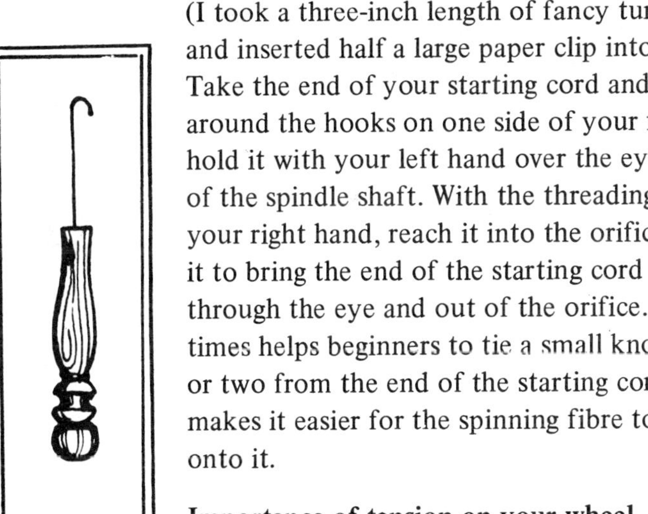

Importance of tension on your wheel. Tension is the amount of pull or tug the wheel puts on the yarn as you spin. You and the wheel should both be pulling at opposite ends of the fibres at the same time. To better understand this, hold a mass of fibres in your right hand. With your left thumb and forefinger, begin pulling out some fibres and twisting them. When you are spinning on the wheel, the action of your left hand pulling and twisting will be performed by the wheel. The amount of tug exerted by your left hand is the same as the amount of tug you will want from the wheel.

While you are spinning, the amount of tension from the wheel should be great enough so that the wheel can literally pull out the fibres from the mass you are holding–and twist them and wind the yarn onto the bobbin. To do this, the wheel needs little or no help from your left hand.

If the tension is too loose, the wheel cannot draw out the fibres and wind them on the bobbin fast enough. As a result, the yarn will overtwist.

If the tension is too tight, it will tug the fibres out of your hand and jerk them into the wheel before they have been twisted sufficiently. This will cause the yarn to drift apart or break.

How to adjust the tension. Tension is created by the differential of revolutions-per-minute between the bobbin and flyer. (In other words: the flyer turns around a little faster, or a little slower, than the bobbin.) Most saxony-style wheels (Finnish, Norwegian, Colonial, Canadian, new wheels now being made in the U.S.) have a doubled drive band. This looks like two string loops, but it is actually one large loop, doubled over. Both loops go around the big wheel at the right. But at the left side, one loop goes around the groove in the whorl, and one loop goes around the groove in the bobbin. If the whorl has two grooves, beginners are advised to put the string in the groove with the larger diameter. This allows you to spin more slowly.

At the left end of the table on most saxony-style wheels, there is a wooden screw. As you turn the screw in one direction, the flyer assembly moves toward the big wheel, and the drive band becomes looser. A loose drive band gives less tension from the wheel. As you turn the screw in the other direction, the flyer assembly moves away from the big wheel, and the drive band becomes tighter. A tight drive band gives more tension from the wheel.

On many castle-style or upright-style wheels, and on the Ashford wheel, there is a single drive band which acts only to rotate the large wheel. There is a knob with a string attached, which goes around the bobbin and connects to a spring or elastic, on the other side of the bobbin (Scotch tension). When this knob is turned in one direction, it loosens the string around the bobbin and reduces the tension. When the knob is turned in the other direction, the string around the bobbin becomes more taut, and the tension therefore increases. At times this can be a very fine adjustment. On some wheels, just turning the knob a quarter-inch can completely alter the tension. If neither the flyer nor the bobbin rotate when you treadle, then this tension cord is too tight. (see the diagram on page 8 showing Scotch tension.)

Play with your tension awhile. Bring your starter cord through the orifice. Adjust your tension very loosely. Now hold the end of the starter cord and treadle a few times. Watch what happens: the yarn twists but it won't wind on. Now adjust the tension very firmly. Again hold the starter cord and treadle several times; this time the yarn should jerk forward and wind on before it is twisted sufficiently. Now, try adjusting the tension at all the stages between very loose and very tight—until you thoroughly get the feeling of what it does.

When you begin spinning various fibres you will find that you *will not need* much tension tug from the wheel if: the fibre is easy to draw apart, if it is slippery, or has a short staple, or if you want to spin a very thin yarn. On the other hand, if the fibre has a long staple, or if it is "in the grease", or if you want to spin a thick yarn—then you *will need* a firm tension tug from the wheel. Note: as the bobbin fills, you will need to increase the tension slightly.

All wheels will spin yarns as thick as their orifice or as fine as sewing thread—if the tension is well adjusted. Tension is the magic that allows your wheel to fully function. And it is probably the single most important thing you can learn about your wheel.

The drawing-out triangle. You must learn to observe what happens in the area where the fibres are being drawn out of the mass, and being twisted. This area usually assumes a somewhat triangular shape. The triangle must be long enough to allow the individual fibres to slide freely past each other as they are being drawn into the twist. So the length of the triangle will change when you change from one fibre to another.

The number of fibres that are in the triangle at any moment determines the thickness of that portion of yarn.

Keep your eyes always on the drawing-out triangle as you spin:

- If the twist runs up too far and the triangle becomes shorter than the length of the staple of fibre, you won't be able to continue drawing back the mass of unspun fibre.
- If you draw the triangle out longer than the length of the staple, the yarn will get thin and drift apart or break.
- If suddenly there are too many fibres in the triangle they will form a lump.
- If suddenly too few fibres are in the triangle, that portion will become thin.

When you understand this, you will find it really very easy to spin anything. There are no "difficult fibres"—only inadequate understanding of them.

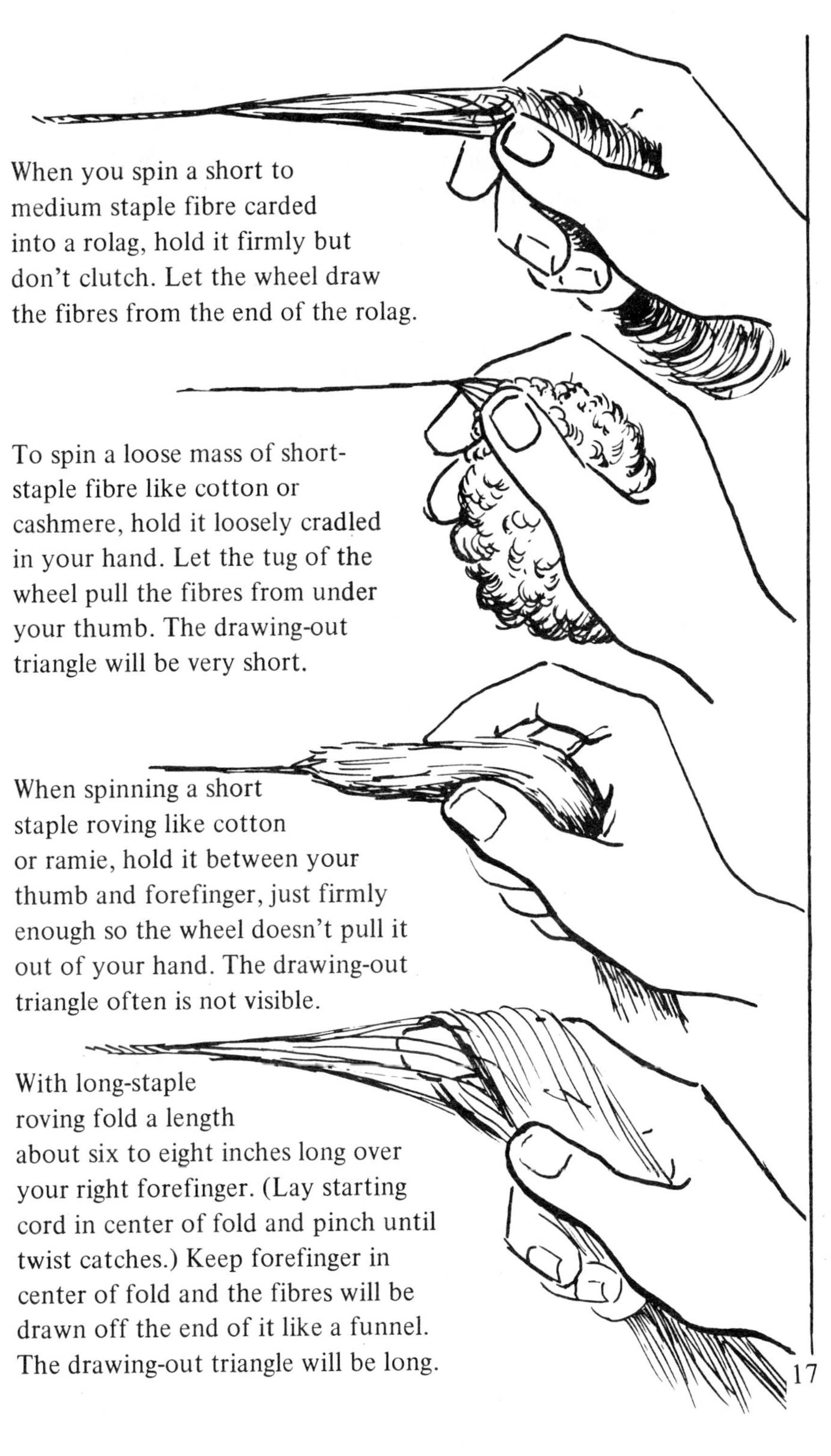

When you spin a short to medium staple fibre carded into a rolag, hold it firmly but don't clutch. Let the wheel draw the fibres from the end of the rolag.

To spin a loose mass of short-staple fibre like cotton or cashmere, hold it loosely cradled in your hand. Let the tug of the wheel pull the fibres from under your thumb. The drawing-out triangle will be very short.

When spinning a short staple roving like cotton or ramie, hold it between your thumb and forefinger, just firmly enough so the wheel doesn't pull it out of your hand. The drawing-out triangle often is not visible.

With long-staple roving fold a length about six to eight inches long over your right forefinger. (Lay starting cord in center of fold and pinch until twist catches.) Keep forefinger in center of fold and the fibres will be drawn off the end of it like a funnel. The drawing-out triangle will be long.

Please don't clutch at the gossamer web. Tightly clutching the unspun mass of fibre is a common problem among beginning spinners. Hold the fibres lightly–just enough so the tug of the wheel doesn't pull the whole mass away from you. If you squeeze them nervously they tend to stick together–a sweaty palm will dampen them–and you will have a matted mess. Fibres draw out more easily if they aren't squeezed. Leave them in a light, loose, airy mass. Tend to cradle the mass toward the back so you do not interfere with the free drawing-out of the fibres.

The same reflex that causes you to clutch, causes you to speed up your treadling when you have a problem. The instant you run into difficulty–stop! . . . Stop treadling, stop clutching! Then examine your drawing-out triangle to determine what happened.

Beginning to spin. Carded wool "in the grease" is probably the easiest fibre for beginners because "dirty" fibres are more cohesive than "clean" fibres. Try to begin with a staple not more than three or four inches long (see section on wool). Hold a comfortable handful (or a rolag) in your right hand. Loosen a small tuft of the mass and lay the starting cord over it–overlapping two or three inches–and pinch this length lightly between the thumb and forefinger of your left hand.

Start treadling your wheel *slowly* clockwise. Watch the twist running up the starting cord. You can feel when it reaches your thumb and forefinger. At that instant you can both see and feel the fibres catch on the starting cord. Continue to hold the "caught" area between the thumb and forefinger. Treadle five or six times, and stop. Draw your right hand back as you release the accumulated twist held by your left hand. Watch the twist run up toward your right hand. Practice this, step-by-step, keeping your eye on the drawing-out triangle.

When you feel confident about each stage, begin to *maintain* a slow, continuous treadling, as your right hand moves backward as fast as the twist runs toward it. Your right hand can make a long, sweeping continuous draw until it reaches arm's length.

To let the yarn wind on, move your right arm forward in a sweeping motion toward the orifice. Allow it to wind on as fast as possible—while still maintaining enough tension to keep the thread straight, not slack. Twist will only run up a *taut* thread.

At first you will need to use your left thumb and forefinger to control the twist and tension a bit, but don't hang on to it as a security blanket. Consciously try to give that left hand less and less to do as you practice. It should be held near the orifice just to guide and smooth the yarn. (I rarely use my left hand, unless I am spinning a very thick yarn. Then I use it to assist the tug from the wheel, and to pull out any slubs.) Left-handed people can reverse these directions.

If your yarn breaks, you will need to join the two ends. The ends will not join if they are tapered and they look like this:

You must fan out the fibres until they look like this:

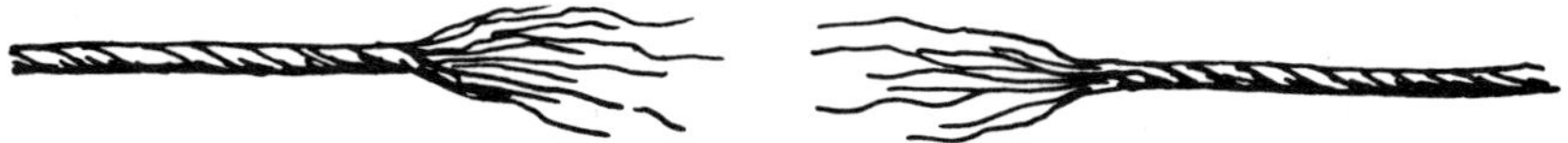

Then overlap the fanned-out ends and hold them between your thumb and forefinger. Treadle until the twist joins them. With a little practice you can make a good join that cannot be seen.

Stumbling blocks—how to overcome them.

- Yarn is overtwisting and looks like a corkscrew.
  - Slow down your treadling, or increase the tension from your wheel. A portion of yarn that is both thin and overtwisted will be brittle.

- Wheel is trying to jerk the yarn out of your hand.
  - Loosen the tension from your wheel.

- The twist runs up and engulfs the whole mass of fibres, and you can't tug it free.
  - You didn't move your hand back rapidly enough. Don't try to tug–you can't draw out fibres that are already twisted. Go back to the area where the yarn began to thicken, and untwist a few inches until it draws freely. Then you can re-spin the remainder. Next time, move your hand back more quickly–or slightly increase the tension of the wheel.

- Yarn is getting thinner and thinner.
  - Don't panic. Just pause, and treadle without moving your hand back. As some twist accumulates it will begin drawing out more fibres from your right hand. Next time, move your right hand back more slowly–or else treadle more rapidly.

- Small lumps.
  - Don't worry about them. They are usually structurally sound and are almost always caused by insufficient carding. To remove them, try rolling them between the thumb and forefinger of your left hand just before they disappear into the orifice.

- Large lumps.
  - Stop treadling. Hold the yarn with a thumb and forefinger at each end of the lump, allowing a distance between your hands at least as long as the staple of the fibre. Untwist until the fibres between your thumbs are all parallel. Then pull out the lump.

- The yarn won't wind on the bobbin.
  - Perhaps the yarn has come off the flyer hooks. This often happens if you treadle the wheel *counter-clockwise.* Unwind the yarn wrapped around the shaft of the spindle and start over. (Be sure the shaft is sufficiently oiled, and the hooks and inside of the orifice are clean.)
  - It is also possible that a single fibre may have caught around one of the flyer hooks. Free it and continue. Some wheels have very tiny hooks. You can take pliers and carefully

unbend them slightly.

– A tighly corkscrewed overtwist may have caught on a flyer hook. Free it.

– There may be a lump squeezed into the orifice. Remember, you can't spin yarn larger than the orifice. Pull the lump back out, untwist and re-spin.

- Flyer does not turn easily.
  – Check to see if the bearings on the front and back maidens are straight. They should be at right angles to the spindle shaft.

- You cannot pull any fibres from your right hand.
  – If the fibres are *parallel* but won't pull apart, it can only be because your hands are too close together, and you are pulling on both ends of the same fibre. Move your hands farther apart.

- The yarn flies off the hooks and billows out as you wind on.
  – This can happen when you begin spinning fast. If you sweep your hand too rapidly toward the orifice when winding on, centrifugal force will send the slack sailing off the hooks in an airborne arc.

Skeining spun yarn. The simplest way to make a skein of yarn is to wind it by encircling your elbow and the "V" between your thumb and forefinger. However, this method does not allow for accurate measuring of yardage. The handiest way to make a skein is with a niddy-noddy – a stick for winding and measuring yarn. You can buy one, or make it with dowels.

If you make your niddy-noddy, be sure that the cross arms that go through the center shaft are set perpendicular to each other. The arms are set 18 inches apart to make a skein a yard long – two yards around. You can measure yardage and weigh skeins to calculate the number of yards for weaving, etc.

If you free the string from around the bobbin groove, you can wind off directly from the bobbin on the spindle shaft onto the

niddy-noddy. Or, many wheels have a built-on bobbin rack, so you can store several bobbins, and then wind off. If your wheel doesn't have a bobbin rack you can buy or make one.

Hold the niddy-noddy in the center with your left hand, and tuck the end of the yarn under your left thumb. Wind around as shown, to form two V-shapes. Use the yarn ends to tie a double half-hitch around each end of the skein. Slip it off the niddy-noddy and onto your forefingers. Rotate the right forefinger clockwise and the left forefinger counter-clockwise, to twist the skein tightly. Put one end through the loop at the other end and it will twist itself into the position shown.

Setting the twist. If your yarn was spun from "fleece in the grease" or other "dirty" fibres, make suds in lukewarm water and wash the skein as you would a sweater, then rinse in water the same temperature. If the fibres you spun were clean, just dip the skein in lukewarm water. A dash of vinegar or lemon juice in the rinse water will make hair fibres shine. Fabric softener or hair creme rinse in the rinse water will give a nice feel to wool and down fibres. Vegetable fibres should be dipped in clear water.

To hang the skeins and set the twist, I use "s" hooks from the hardware, and lead fishing weights sold by the ounce. Always remove the weight as soon as the twist is set or the yarn is dry, so it does not deaden the resilience of the yarn. The amount of weight should be greater than that of the yarn. For instance, a four-ounce skein should have at least a six-ounce weight.

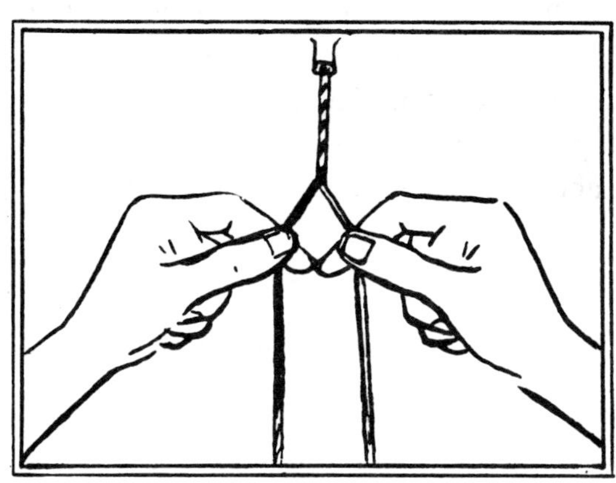

Plying. If you intend to ply yarn, your single strands should be spun with a slight overtwist to compensate for the amount of untwisting that occurs when you ply. Put two full bobbins on your bobbin caddy. If you don't have one, put the bobbins on a knitting needle stuck through a shoe box. The important thing is for the bobbins to turn easily and evenly. Set it at your feet under the orifice. Take an end of yarn from each bobbin and tie them to the starting cord.

Adjust your tension screw so there will be a firm tug from the wheel. Hold one thread in each hand. Brace your forefingers together if you want an even ply. Treadle *counter* clockwise as you let the yarn move freely through your hands. If you are plying more than two threads at once, slip a finger between each thread to keep the yarns separated. If you want an uneven ply, hold one thread more tautly and the other will wrap around it.

Reasons for plying: Plying increases strength. By making a two or three-ply yarn, you can increase thickness. You can ply colors together to make a "tweed" yarn. You can also ply two types of fibre together, but make sure their physical properties (such as shrinkage) are compatible. Plied yarn will "pill" less than singles.

A word about the anatomy of yarn.

Warp yarn: Don't be afraid to spin warp yarns. If they have a good twist they will not present any problems. Remember, weavers have used handspun warp for 7,000 years. It is important that the yarn be evenly, smoothly and tightly spun – and that the twist be well set. Allow for more shrinkage on a tightly twisted yarn. I do not use sizing on warp, and I have spun and woven fine single-strand unsized cashmere and camel down warp without any breakage.

Weft yarn: Any structurally sound yarn can be spun – tight or loose, smooth or lumpy. A loosely twisted yarn will have less weight in relation to its bulk, and less shrinkage.

Lumps: To be structurally sound a lump must be shorter than the average staple length of the fibre. For instance, if your staple is an inch long, the lump shouldn't be an inch and a half long, or the fibres in the center area of the lump won't be twisted:

So your lumps in cotton, cashmere and camel down must be quite small. In a long-staple fibre, they can be as long as you like.

Knitting yarn: If you begin knitting from the starting end of handspun yarn it won't "pill" as much as if you start from the other end (it is like rubbing a dog's fur the wrong way). When skeining off knitting yarn, tie a colored string to the end near the starting cord; and knit from this end.

NATURAL FIBRES

We are now participating in a renaissance in aesthetics – a rediscovery of the look and feel of the natural world. A generation was born into a world dominated by plastics and synthetic fabrics. Senses are dulled by smooth, slick machine-made objects for living. Now there is a reawakening of sensory perception – a renewed enjoyment of the subtle variations in natural materials – and an effort to reintegrate natural textures into our lives.

Don't limit your spinning to wool, or you will miss much of the fun of spinning. Every fibre has its own distinct personality. Approach each as a new adventure. Experiment with blending various fibres, and you can design yarn specifically for the use you plan. A far wider range will be available to you than is commercially offered. It is often easier to spin yarn than to shop for it – it is certainly more enjoyable.

Spinners in other cultures have been mostly limited to fibres produced locally. Throughout history, the search for new fibres and textiles has been one of the causes for exploration, discovery and conquest. Now we are the first people to have nearly every fibre from all over the world imported and easily accessible to us.

Most of the fibres on the following pages are sold by the fleece, the pound or the ounce. Many are sold in loose masses which often need no carding or special treatment before spinning. Alpaca, mohair, camel, goat, yak, silk, linen, cotton, jute and hemp are among the fibres sold in combed form ready to spin. Combed fibres are called "top," "roving," "sliver" and other names. Usage depends on process and area, and varies between industry and handspinners. I will use "roving" here.

WOOL

Since the late Stone Age, people have used wool. 6,000 years ago in ancient Babylon and Mesopotamia people wore wool garments and traded fleeces. The British have worn wool clothing for 5,000 years.

The Roman conquests spread the spinning and weaving of wool throughout Europe and their far-flung empire. During the middle ages there was great competition in wool raising. England and Spain produced the most and the finest. After the defeat of Spain, England ruled the wool markets, and the strength of the Empire was built on the wool trade.

Queen Elizabeth I established the custom of all nobles kneeling on a sack of wool while they swore loyalty to the Crown. This was to serve as a reminder that their power and position were founded on wool.

The first sheep that discovered America arrived on the Santa Maria with Columbus. Sheep brought by the conquistadores eventually ranged over the lands of the Mexicans, the Navajos and Pueblos. By 1633 the Massachusetts Bay Colony received their first sheep. A few years later they passed a law that every family had to produce three pounds of wool, cotton or linen a month, or pay a fine. A spinning wheel cost three shillings.

Now, wool is produced throughout the world, with these countries leading: Australia, Russia, New Zealand, Argentina, South Africa.

Wool is a protein fibre that somewhat resembles human hair. However, under the microscope we can see that the outer layer is covered with overlapping scales – 1,000 to 3,000 per inch. These scales open or close slightly when subjected to temperature changes. They give cohesion to the wool as you spin it. Wool is remarkably elastic. It can absorb up to 30% of its weight in water and still feel dry to the touch. The molecular arrangement of wool begins to break down at 212° F. This is why we steam press wool to "block" it. The heat and moisture rearrange the molecular structure, and the wool assumes the new shape we give it.

Sheep breeds. There are over 200 breeds of sheep in the world. Fleeces average less than ten pounds. Some weigh as little as two pounds, and a Lincoln ram was shorn of a record 46½ pounds. They are graded by length of fibres, diameter (15 to 70 microns), and crimp (natural wave). They are creamy white, coal black and all the shades of grey and brown. Depending on age and breed, the staple can be from one and a half inches to a record of 32 inches.

There are short wool and down breeds that look like this. They grow a fine, springy, tightly-crimped fleece and tend to live in lowlands and wooded areas under 1,000 ft. altitudes where pasture is good and rainfall is high. Staple is about two to five inches. Most down breeds are good for woolen spinning. Typical breeds are Corriedale, Columbia, Rambouillet, Hampshire and Suffolk.

There are long wool and lustre breeds that are covered with long, shaggy ringlets. Their fleece tends to be coarse but very strong and lustrous. They live in rich grasslands and coastal plains. Staple is commonly six to twelve inches and is excellent for worsted spinning. Breeds include Lincoln, Leicester, Romney Marsh and Ripon.

There are highland breeds that usually have long, hairy (kempy) fleece and under down. They have a coarse staple with little crimp. They generally live in high rocky hills and plateaus at altitudes of 1,000 ft. or more. Karakul, although its staple is not as long, falls into this group. Most common are Rough Fell, Scottish Blackface and Swaledale.

Selecting fleece. Unless you have been spinning for some time and really know good fleece, *don't* buy fleece from a local farmer. Go to or write to a store that sells fleece for handspinners. There are many throughout the country. In any case, don't buy raw fleece that is really dirty, matted and full of seeds and burrs. In no way is it worth it.

Much of our best handspinning wool we owe to the spread of the British Empire – for the sheep trade followed the English to Australia, New Zealand, and South Africa. They have a tradition of good management of their flocks. The fleece is better cared for and of higher quality than in other countries. They often rinse the sheep a few days before shearing, so it is cleaner.

I rarely buy fleece that needs washing before it is spun. And I try to get fleece in such good condition that I can spin it without carding. At a higher price it is a better bargain. Remember, you're paying for the dirt in the fleece along with the wool.

Shearing is usually done in the spring in the U.S. and in the fall south of the equator. A good shearer can shear a fleece in one piece that looks like a sheepskin when it is laid out. Traditionally it has been folded in thirds and rolled, starting from the tail, toward the neck. The neck portion was pulled out, twisted and tied around the rolled fleece to hold it together. When you see a fleece like this, the shorn side is always folded outward, so it appears clean and free of dirt and burrs. Pinch a small piece and sharply tug it out of the fleece to examine its condition. Pull the lock to be sure it is strong. If the sheep has had poor pasture, has been sick, or pregnant without food supplements, the lock will break. If this happens, don't buy it.

Sorting and storing raw fleeces. Unless you have at least three or four fleeces, it doesn't make sense to sort them in the traditional way. Just lay out your fleece on the floor. Pull off any short staple patches around the edges. Throw away any bits of barnyard. Remove any very hairy patches – like around the tail. Mix the rest together and package in plastic bags, and store in a dark, cool, dry place (I use trash cans). The shorter time it is stored, the better. Never store more than six months before spinning. Old wool "in the grease" becomes stiff and harsh and is hard to spin. Freshly shorn fleece is soft and supple. I urge beginners to buy fleece by the pound, not by the whole fleece – and to buy from a reputable handspinning supply store where the fleece is fresh.

About moths. If you should ever have wool with moths in it, there are three things you can do: You can put it in an airtight bag with moth balls or crystals (this however is no longer always effective – sometimes the eggs wait to hatch until conditions are favorable). You can soak the wool in water overnight – this will drown them. Or, if you have a sufficiently large freezer, you can freeze the wool for several days.

Raw wool vs. clean wool. Raw wool, called "fleece in the grease", comes directly from the sheep to you. The lanolin ("grease") is still in it. It has all the bounce and resilience characteristic of wool. There is a very rewarding feeling and a fine sense of accomplishment when you perform all the steps necessary to convert a raw fleece into finished skeins of handspun yarn. Here are some reasons why you should buy raw wool:

- You must buy raw wool if you want to use most of the interesting breeds that are raised throughout the world. Clean wool is available to handspinners only in a few breeds, and usually only in white.
- You must buy raw wool if you want to blend shades together. Many of the grey, brown and black breeds grow fleeces of softly varying colors that are full of surprises. Remember, the colors will change when they are washed. A yellow-grey will usually become a silver-grey.
- When you blend another fibre with raw wool, the lanolin will help to "hold" the other fibre.
- Raw wool, even when carefully hand-processed, retains more of its original character.

Clean wool, often called scoured wool, has all the lanolin and dirt removed. It is sometimes available uncombed, but more often in roving form. It usually costs a little more, but is more economical because there is no weight loss – as much as a third of the weight of raw wool can be washed out. When you use roving, it is relatively easy to spin an even, structurally sound yarn. And if you are in a hurry, you don't have to spend time carding and washing. Roving is available commercially prepared in a long coil of clean, combed fibres. The fibres are aligned and it will produce a more compact, smooth-surface yarn than a rolag. (If you want to make a more airy yarn, pull it apart with your fingers to form a fluffy mass.)

Washing wool. Unless you have an excellent reason, please don't buy wool that is so dirty as to need washing before you spin it. If you insist on getting it, this is what you do:

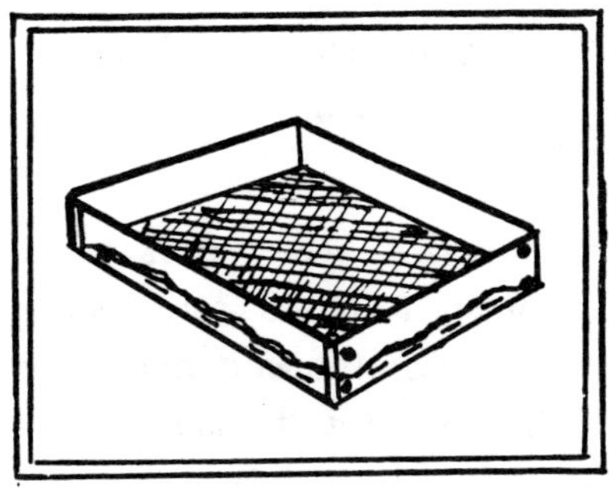

1. **Container.** If you have just a little wool, you can use a kitchen colander. If you have a lot, nail four boards together to make a frame slightly smaller than your sink or tub. Staple a piece of nylon net over the bottom. About a pound of wool is right for the average kitchen sink. Pull the wool apart with your hands so there are no densely matted clumps.

2. If you want to remove both the dirt and grease (grease must be removed if you plan to dye it), use water warmer than your skin, and a big dash of liquid detergent. If you want to remove the dirt but not all the lanolin, use cool water and a generous amount of mild soap flakes. The suds should never go "flat" while the wool is being washed.

3. Make the sudsy solution in the sink. *Never* run water directly on the wool.

4. Set the box of wool in the sink and press the wool gently but firmly down to the bottom to let all the air bubbles escape.

5. Let it sit and soak for 15 minutes to overnight – depending on how dirty it is. You may need to put it through two washings. The water will be very dirty.

6. When it has soaked long enough, lift out the box and the dirty water will run through the nylon net bottom, but the wool itself will not escape and clog the drain.

7. Run your rinse water into the sink at the same temperature

as the water which just ran down the drain. Submerge the box of wool – very gently press down the fleece. Lift out the box. Drain, and run new water, repeating the process until the water remains clear and clean.

8. In the final rinse I put in a dash of cream hair rinse. This helps ease the tangles – in wool as in human hair – and makes carding easier.

9. Lift the box of wool out of the final rinse and carry it outdoors. Prop it against something or set it off the ground so air can circulate through the bottom. Loosen the wool mass and lightly pull it apart. If the wool is white, set it in the shade; prolonged exposure to sun will darken white wool. When it is almost dry, begin teasing and fluffing it.

10. The most important things to remember when washing raw wool: Make your soap solution first, and don't run the water on the wool. Don't squeeze, wring, stir or agitate it any more than necessary. *Never, never* transfer it to hotter or colder water than it was just removed from!

Oiling. After the washed wool has been carded, you may want to add some oil for easier spinning. You can buy lanolin spinning oil and spray this on the wool. Vegetable oils work well but turn rancid in a short time. If you do use them, spin the wool as soon as possible after oiling. Leave the oiled wool in a warm place, so the oil will disperse through the wool. All wool that has been oiled should be washed after it has been spun.

Washing skeins. Wool spun in the grease should be washed the same way as a wool sweater. Use lukewarm water and a liquid detergent. Gently squeeze, but don't wring. Rinse in the same temperature water. I put a dash of lemon juice in the rinse water – or vinegar or fabric softener.

Examine the staple of your fleece. The "staple" is a few strands pulled from the mass to determine the average length, texture and crimp of the fibre. If it looks like this:

. . . it is a downy wool and can produce a soft, fluffy and springy yarn. The individual fibres don't lay closely together in the yarn. There will be many tiny air pockets, so it will be warm.

If your staple looks like this:

. . . it is probably a longwool-lustre and can produce a more compact yarn. The staples will lay closely together. It will be heavier, smoother and more lustrous. It will not "pill" as quickly as a softer yarn.

Carding. Historically, carding was done with thistles (teasels). Its name comes from the Latin "cardusis", meaning thistle. Our use of the word "tease", meaning to pull apart, comes from teasel. Carders are two wooden brushes. They have a covering pad of leather or vinyl set with bent wire teeth. I prefer the leather covering. Run your thumb over the teeth in the same direction as the wire is bent. It should feel somewhat soft and flexible.

Store your carders with a pad of raw wool between them. This will keep the leather soft and the teeth will not rust. Write "left" on one carder and "right" on the other, and always use them that way. As you card, pick out any debris, short little double-cuts or burrs, etc.

If the wool does not pull apart easily, tease it before you start carding. To do this, spread the locks apart between your fingers, so that no tangles remain which could damage the teeth of the carders.

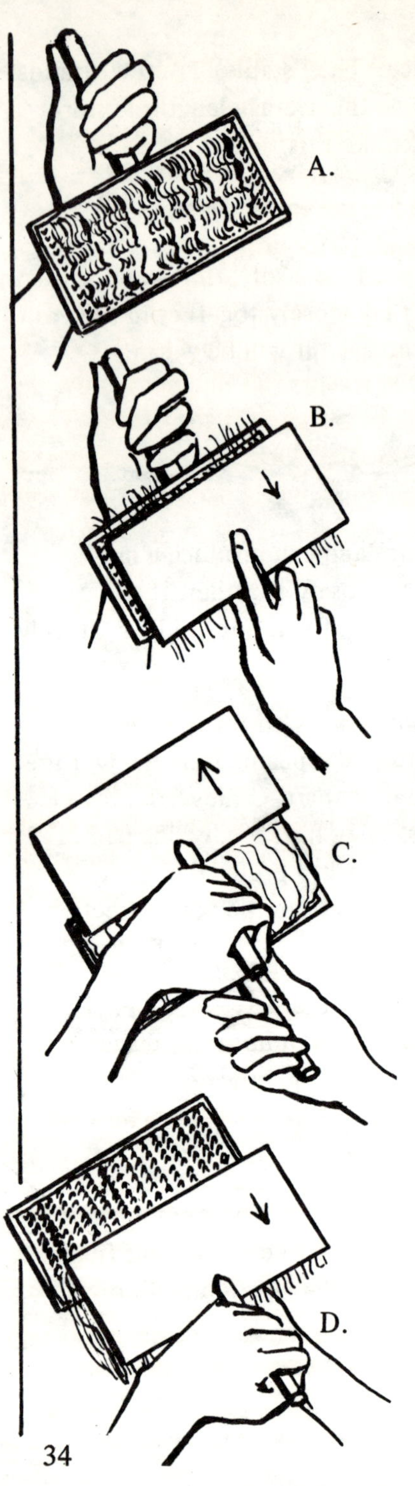

A. Hold the left carder firmly braced on your knee. Spread a handful of teased wool locks on it with the shorn end of the locks at the top edge of the carder.

B. Firmly grasp the other carder in your right hand and lay it on the center of the left carder and lightly brush the right carder toward you. Make a long stroke out to the full length of the wool. Do this several times until the fibres begin to align.

C. Lay the right carder on your knee and hold it firmly in your right hand. Hold the left carder with the handle pointing toward you, and brush it *away* from you over the right carder. This will deposit all the wool on the *right* carder. Brush a few times.

D. Lay the right carder on your knee and hold it firmly in your right hand. Hold the left carder with the handle pointing toward you over the right carder, and brush it *toward* you over the right carder. This will deposit all the wool on the *left* carder. Now brush it a few times.

Continue this procedure until both sides of the wool look well brushed.

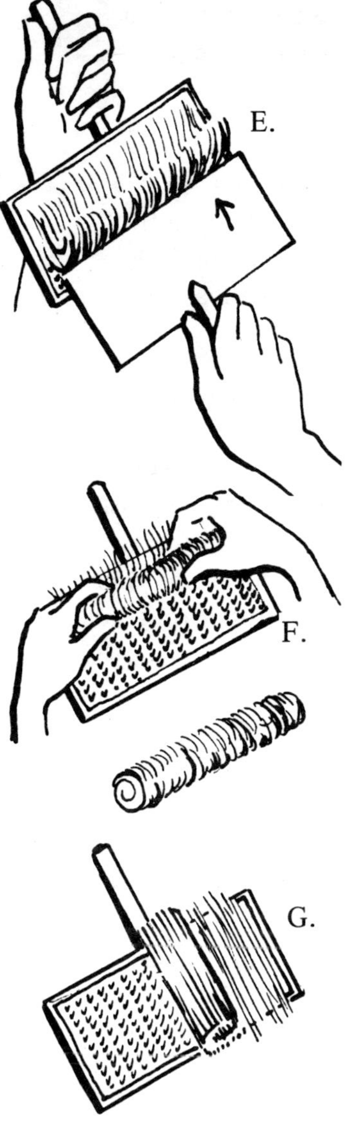

E. Now deposit all the wool on the left carder. Use the right carder to brush up the edge of the wool pad, to loosen it.

F. Lay the left carder on your lap (handle outward) and with all ten fingers roll the pad firmly outward and off the carder. This is called a "rolag". It is for a short to medium staple wool that you want to spin into a wooly yarn. When this is spun the fibres will not lay parallel to each other within the yarn. The yarn will be bouncy, light, resilient and fuzzy. This is traditionally called woolen spinning.

G. If you are working with a long staple wool, roll or fold the wool pad across the carder. Spin the pad lengthwise from the end. When spun this way, the fibres will lay parallel to each other and the yarn will be smoother, more lustrous and compact. This is used for what is traditionally called "worsted spinning".

Things to avoid in carding:

Don't worry about the carding sequence. It is not important to remember, so don't be confused by it. The thing to remember is that the wool should be brushed and turned over from one carder, and then brushed and turned over from the other carder. This is so both layers of the wool are brushed on both sides (otherwise you will have an unbrushed layer lurking in there somewhere).

Don't make a fetish of carding. Don't over-card. Carded wool is easier for a beginner to spin – but fleeces in good condition can be spun into beautiful yarns without any carding. If the wool is relatively clean, you can simply spread it apart and tease it with your fingers before you spin it.

Don't make itty-bitty rolags the size of your finger. Do put as much wool on the carder as you can manage – you should be able to feel the wire teeth just very lightly touching each other when you brush. I make rolags firmly rolled, an inch and a half to two inches in diameter. Remember, you can damage your carders if you use them too roughly. Brush firmly but lightly.

Don't make an unmanageably loose rolag. As you roll it off, tuck in any wool that is drifting off the sides of the carder when it is rolled. If the rolag is too airy, it will drift apart as you spin.

Combing. If your wool has a staple more than six inches long, it is difficult to manage on hand carders. However, this can be combed. Clamp a worsted comb to the edge of a table (if you can't obtain one, a dog comb or a wide-tooth metal comb will do). Hold the shorn end of a wool lock and pull the tip through the teeth of the comb. Turn the wool lock around and hold it by the tip to comb out the shorn end.

Drum carder. Don't expect a drum carder to do all the work for you. It really doesn't make carding *that* much easier. Raw wool must be thoroughly teased (using your fingers to open the matted areas) before feeding it into the drum carder. Often the wool must be put through the drum carder several times before it is sufficiently carded. To remove the carded wool, take a sturdy knitting needle or ice pick, etc. Slide it carefully across the cylinder on the channel where the carding cloth is joined together. Lift the wool until it separates. It will then roll off the drum in a large bat about a foot wide by two feet long. This can be divided lengthwise to make several strips of roving. Or it can be divided across and rolled into rolags. It is designed more to be used for worsted-type spinning, rather than woolen.

I use my drum carder almost exclusively for blending. It works perfectly for this. For instance, I will feed in alternate handfulls of light and dark colored fibres – turn it several times – and it produces a beautifully streaked color mix.

When not in use, leave a bat of raw wool on the cylinder of the carder to protect the leather and wire teeth. Remember to clean and oil it often. Be careful to not allow fibres to wrap themselves around the axles of the cylinders.

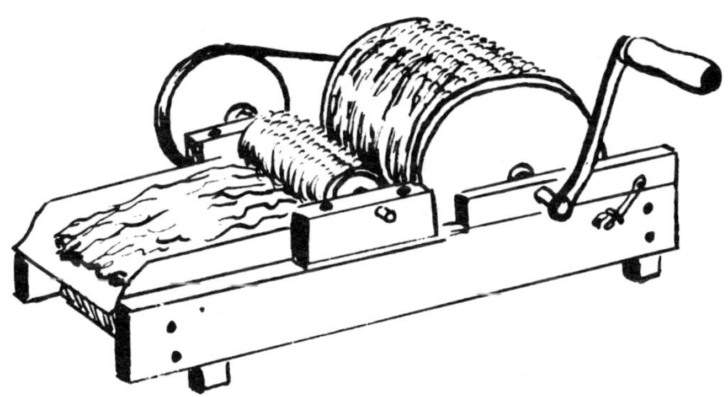

Blending different fibres together. Try blending two fibres. This should be done when you want to add strength – as when you add wool to samoyed. Or when you want to give a longer wearing quality – as when you add camel hair to wool. Or when you want a special effect – such as blending glistening white mohair into a dark shade of wool.

You can blend fibres on hand carders. For example, let's take wool and camel hair. You will use half as much wool as usual (since you will fill in with camel hair). Think in terms of making a sandwich. Put the wool on the left carder and give it several brushes with the right carder, so there is a pad of wool on each carder (these are the two slices of bread). Now sprinkle the camel hair across the left carder (this is the sandwich filling). Brush the right carder over it and proceed to card and make a rolag as you would with plain wool. The reason for this procedure is so the camel hair won't sink down to the bottom of the carding teeth. As you begin to card, the wool has already enveloped the loose camel hair. In general, put the longest most cohesive fibres on the carder first, and the shortest, most slippery fibres second.

Such a mixture of wool and camel hair is too coarse to wear next to your skin, but it makes a beautiful long-wearing yarn for rugs. It bulks up the wool. When it is spun and washed, the camel tends to free itself partly from the core of the wool, and forms a golden brown halo around it.

When blending different fibres on the drum carder, follow the same procedure. After the first layer of wool, alternately add hair and wool. But also remove the bat and run it through the carder several times to mix the two types of fibres sufficiently.

You will learn a lot about fibres if you try this experiment: Begin by carding a rolag containing about 90% of the first fibre and 10% of the second. Now work your way up the scale until your last rolag consists of about 10% of the first type of fibre and 90% of the second. When you spin this pile of rolags, you will understand what blending can do.

ALPACA

The alpaca, llama, guanaco and vicuña are all members of the South American Camel Family. Alpaca were domesticated and used as a beast of burden since ancient times in the highlands of Peru and Bolivia, and can live above 12,000 ft. altitudes.

The ancient Peruvians produced the finest weaving of alpaca. They spun it into weft yarn only, and wove it on cotton warp. They were able to spin two-ply that measured 168,000 yards per pound. This means they were able to spin single-strand alpaca at a truly amazing 191 miles per pound. The spinning was done on a hand-spindle which is capable of making a much finer thread than a spinning wheel. The very finest alpaca can have a staple so thin that you cannot see a single fibre when you lay it on a sheet of white paper. When trying to duplicate this feat, I have spun thread as fine as human hair – but this is much coarser than the Peruvian handspun.

Since Peru and Bolivia are below the equator, the animals are shorn in December. They are small – about three and a half feet high at the shoulder. Many fleeces are brought to the large central market in Arequipa, Peru. There are now an estimated half a million alpacas.

Alpaca is stronger than wool and, like wool, fibres from different parts of the body vary in thickness. The finest breed is the suri, whose silky fleece hangs to the ground and measures up to 20 inches long. Cross-breeding has produced the huarizo, from a female alpaca and a male llama; and the misti, from a male alpaca and a female llama. The range of natural alpaca colors is wide: snowy white, silvery blue-greys, true black, rose beige, cinnamon brown, and brown-black.

Spinning alpaca. Alpaca is a good fibre to try after wool. You can get raw alpaca in fleeces or by the pound. I weighed 15 fleeces and they all weighed around three to four pounds, so that might be average. There is little waste, since there is no grease to lose in washing, and almost the entire fleece is usable. It will be easier to use if the animal was brushed prior to shearing. If you are looking for a very fine and softly crimped alpaca, you are more likely to find it in raw fleeces. Good raw alpaca needs only a light carding with wool carders, or once around on a drum carder. Spin it as you would spin wool of the same length staple.

Many stores also carry alpaca in roving form. The commercially prepared roving tends to be the tiniest bit heavier and coarser than raw fleece. You can lightly card two colors together and blend endless variations. To spin alpaca roving, pull out a few hairs to check the length of the staple (it should be *at least* six inches, probably longer). This means you will have a long drawing-out triangle. Remember to hold a length of the roving over your forefinger. Don't let the twist run up too far into the triangle, or the fibres won't slide past each other and the yarn will immediately thicken. You will need a firm – but not jerking – takeup from your wheel. (see diagram on page 17)

Alpaca is quite strong and unless you are spinning a warp, it won't need much twist – just enough to hold the yarn together. Alpaca compresses easily, so an overtwist will produce a wiry yarn. Keep it loose and furry.

When you have skeined it off, wash and rinse it even if it is "clean" roving. Clean alpaca roving is not always completely clean and can smell like a wet dog. I put a dash of fabric softener or cream hair rinse in the last rinse water – it will feel and smell better. Hang and weight the skein to set the twist. I have never seen alpaca shrink, so do not worry about that.

To get a furry finish when you weave alpaca, brush it with a hair brush from side to side along the weft while you have tension on the loom. Knitted alpaca can be lightly brushed after the knitting has been blocked.

GUANACO

The guanaco is sometimes domesticated but is more often found in the wild in Tierra del Fuego. There it is hunted by the Ona Indians, who wear headdresses resembling the head of the guanaco, and infiltrate the herd with bows and arrows. They eat the meat and use the skins to make their huts, clothes, moccasins and water bags. The surplus fur is sold to commercial buyers.

The guanaco staple is shorter than alpaca, and the softest fibres come from the young animals (called guanacitos), and are a creamy honey beige. Because the guanacos are usually killed for their pelts, I urge handspinners not to seek it out. Perhaps domestication will become more successful and widespread, and it will then be on the market for handspinners.

LLAMA

The llama is also a member of the Camel Family. It is more numerous than the alpaca. The fleece measures 27 microns (a micron is one-millionth of a meter – and a meter is 39.4 inches). Llama has more uniformity than alpaca. The fibre is often interchangeable with alpaca, and can be spun in the same way.

VICUÑA

Vicuñas, native to southern Peru, live in 16,000 to 19,000 ft. altitudes. They are wild and are killed to obtain the fibre. Because of the demands of the fashion industry, they were hunted almost to extinction by the 1950's. Now they are under Peruvian government protection.

Even if you are able to find black market vicuña, don't buy it. They are small, graceful animals with poufs of fur above their front legs. They are a rich cinnamon brown, shading to lighter on the underside. The average fibre is 13 microns. Fortunately, the hair of all members of the Camel Family cannot be successfully bleached, so they are always left in their own beautiful colors.

MOHAIR

Mohair is the hair shorn from the Angora goat. The word mohair comes from the Arabic word "mukhayyar", meaning "best" or "finest". It was first domesticated in Ankara, Turkey. The earliest European record of mohair is in 1554, when a Flemish diplomat bought two angora goats and presented them to King Charles V of Spain. In 1838 it was introduced into South Africa, and is now also thriving in the southwest U.S.

Mohair grows four to six inches in six months. It is very silky, very lustrous and very strong. The hair can be very fine or coarse. Kid mohair can be almost as fine as cashmere, and other mohair can be ten times thicker. When hand washed, teased and fluffed, it looks like the "angel hair" on Christmas trees.

Raw mohair. If you buy raw mohair in good condition, it washes easily. It may look greyish or yellowish, but is snowy white when washed. Even when dirty, you should be able to pull it apart with your hands. If it is too matted, don't buy it. If the mohair is very dirty, soak it overnight in warm water and washing soda. Then wash and rinse it. Hay and other debris will float away with the rinse water. Raw mohair sometimes has flakes of dry oil. They may not wash out, but they will card out. When the mohair is almost dry (or completely dry), tease it and fluff it apart with your fingers, and it's ready to spin. If it doesn't fall apart easily as you fluff it, you may need to card it lightly; but I've never found this necessary.

If the staple is fine, spin a thinner, fluffier yarn. If it is coarse, spin a heavier, tighter yarn. You will need just slightly less tension on your wheel than for wool. The surface of the fibre is smooth, so you will want a little more twist. After you spin a few yards, test the strength of the yarn. If it's weak, add twist – but if it's strong, decrease the amount of twist. This is because mohair tends to compress. My favorite way to spin mohair is to blend it with wool of a darker shade. It adds strength and resilience. The blend is easy to spin. The mohair partly frees itself from the wool and gives the yarn a silky, glistening surface. Mohair blends easily with almost any fibre.

After spinning, dip it in lukewarm water and weight the skein. Mohair takes dye well.

Mohair roving. This is available in a wide range of natural colors – white to black, greys and browns. It's commercially cleaned and combed (and sometimes dyed). I don't think its texture is as soft or lustrous as good raw mohair – but it is less trouble to use.

Spin it as you would other roving (see diagram on page 17), but don't put any more twist on it than is absolutely necessary to make an adequately strong yarn. It's easy to overtwist mohair – and this makes a heavy, wiry yarn. You will need a little less tension from your wheel than you do with wool – because the mohair fibres are not as cohesive as wool. Skein off and dip in warm water. The roving is often dusty, and this will brighten the highlights. Hang with weights to dry.

Fabrics with some mohair content don't tend to wrinkle. However, most mohair is heavy, and a sweater knitted from pure mohair could weigh twice as much as one of wool. If, when weaving, you alternate areas of pure wool and pure mohair, remember the mohair will not "take up" as much as wool.

CASHMERE

The moment you touch a cloud of unspun cashmere, you will know why it has always been rare and precious. Spinning and weaving cloth of cashmere is an ancient craft in Kashmir, northern India. Their weaving was sent to Rome and was treasured by the Caesars. Cashmere shawls were brought to the courts of Europe in the sixteenth century. They were so light and finely spun, a large shawl could be drawn through a wedding ring.

Cashmere is the soft underdown of the Kashmir goat which is found in Tibet, Iran, Mongolia, northern India and Turkestan. It thrives at altitudes between 12,000 and 15,000 ft. The goats at the highest altitudes produce the finest, softest cashmere. Mongolian and Iranian cashmere are available through hand-spinning stores. The Mongolian costs more and is a better quality than the Iranian. The Kashmir goat, like the camel, produces a double coat yielding two distinctly different fibres – soft underdown, and coarse guard hair. The drawing shows how this appears under the microscope. When the goat sheds in the spring, the down is combed out. One goat yields only three to four ounces of down. The down measures 15 microns or less and has a staple up to three inches long. Unspun down looks like a softly colored cloud and the staple is difficult to see without a

magnifying glass. The hairs measure about 140 microns and have a staple up to five inches. The hair is sold as a separate fibre, and produces a coarse, bristly yarn (this spins like camel hair; see directions under "camel").

When you price cashmere, remember how light it is. Take a big pouf in one hand and drop it into the other hand – you may not feel it land. A pound of cashmere goes much farther than a pound of wool. I weave large 80-inch cashmere shawls that weigh less than five ounces – and full-length cashmere caftans that weigh less than a pound.

The down is clean and needs no carding. Just fluff up a handful and hold it very lightly as you spin. *Don't* clutch it. Lay the starting cord into the edge of the cloud and lightly pinch a few fibres around it, between your thumb and forefinger, until you feel the fibres catch hold of the cord. The drawing-out triangle will usually be too small to see easily. Work with loose tension. The tug should be just enough to allow the yarn to wind on the bobbin. As the twist runs up the yarn, let it go clear up to the mass of fibres. The twist will seem to "eat" the fibres as it pulls them from the mass. (see diagram on page 17).

Hold just a little pressure with the end of your thumb or thumbnail against the side of your forefinger, and let just enough down escape. If you pinch too tightly, the yarn will go thin. If you pinch too loosely, a lump will slip past under your thumb. Your other three fingers shouldn't clutch the cloud of fibres, but should only cradle them enough to keep them from dropping.

If you have problems with breakage, loosen the wheel tension. This will add twist, and down fibres need a lot of twist. Until washed and set they will appear overtwisted, even though they are spun just right. Cashmere (and camel down) produce the most structurally sound yarn when spun from 1,500 to 3,000 yards to the pound. It is difficult to spin them consistently finer on the wheel (it is possible to spin them much finer, though, on a handspindle) and if they are thicker, the staple is too short to have an adequate twist.

When the skeins are wound they should look evenly overtwisted. If you let go of both ends of the skein, it will ball up and look like an Afro wig. Just dip the skein in lukewarm water and hang it with rather a heavy weight. For instance, a four-ounce skein of 300 to 400 yards: half-pound weight. A four-ounce skein of 700 to 800 yards: a one-pound weight (the number of strands in the skein is a determining factor in how much weight is needed). Remember to remove the weight as soon as the twist is set.

There will be some shrinkage, but it will depend on the amount of twist you've put into the yarn. In weaving, I allow two to three inches for each yard wide of weaving.

MUSK OX

The musk ox lives in the Arctic in North America and Greenland. It is not an ox. In many ways it resembles the buffalo and is about two-thirds the size of a buffalo. The Eskimos call it "oomingmak", meaning the "bearded one". It grows a very thick, long coat of brownish black hair that reaches nearly to the ground. In this fur is an undercoat of very fine, soft brown down resembling cashmere, which is called qiviut and which is shed in the spring. Since 1954 there has been a project to reestablish the musk ox in Alaska. When and if qiviut does appear for sale, you can follow the spinning directions for cashmere.

CAMEL

The camel once roamed the entire world except Australia. The camels of today are descended from the stock domesticated by the Babylonians about 1,000 B.C. Our camel down comes from the two-humped Bactrian camel, named for Bactria, an ancient land which is now Afghanistan. Bactrian camels formed the caravans of the Old Silk Road. The Bactrian grows a double coat, a soft layer of underdown amid thick hair. It is found in Mongolia, China and central Asia. Traditionally, people in the caravan were assigned to walk behind the camels and gather the down as it fell to the ground. Sometimes the camels are shorn, and then the hair is separated from the down.

Camel down closely resembles cashmere; the staple is just the slightest bit less fine and silky, and is often mistaken for cashmere. It measures about 17 microns. Since it cannot be bleached successfully, it comes in its natural, beautiful color. Camel down is spun exactly like cashmere in every respect (see directions for spinning cashmere).

Camel hair comes in a variety of diameters and staple lengths, depending on the part of the body on which it grows. The short hair is usually sold in a loose mass. The longer hair is combed into rovings. Camel hair has been used in the Mideast to stuff mattresses. It is also used to make industrial belts because it is unaffected by oil and grease.

Short camel hair has a staple of about two to three inches. Adjust a firm (but not really tight) tension from the wheel. Take a handful of hair and hold it firmly enough so the hairs don't drift away. These fibres are smooth and bristly, so even if you clutch them, they won't compress and mat. Lay the starting cord into the edge of the mass and pinch some fibres around it. Treadle until you feel it join very firmly. The drawing-out triangle will be short. Put on as much twist as you can – without actually letting it kink into an overtwist. This is necessary to make it strong.

When you begin to weave with it, if there are insufficiently spun sections they will drift apart. The fibres are smooth and slippery (like human hair) and only the twist holds them together. When you skein off, dip the skein in lukewarm water. If there is debris mixed into the hair, swish it around in the water and it will mostly rinse out.

Since you have put on a strong twist, you will need to use a heavy weight – up to a pound on a four-ounce skein, or enough to stretch out the kinks. Camel hair is easy to card with wool, and they make a beautiful blend. It bulks up the wool, adds color and when washed, partly frees itself from the twist – making a halo effect around the wool.

Camel hair roving. This has a longer staple, is easier to spin, and produces a stronger yarn. It does cost more than loose camel hair. It will not be quite as bristly and textured as the short hair. Fold it over your forefinger (see diagram on page 17) and spin with a long drawing-out triangle. It is not as cohesive as wool, so put on more twist than with wool. If it is going to be strong it must also be somewhat wiry. Finish it the same as the short camel hair.

Camel hair is scratchy next to your skin – but it can be used for outer garments. Its texture and durability are ideal for rugs and hangings. It does not shrink; if woven with wool, selvages may "wave".

GOAT

Goats are pastured throughout the world for meat, milk and hair. They have been here since the Pleistocene Epoch – about a million years. The Bezoar goat of Iran is said to be the ancestor species of our domestic goat. Goats are among the hardiest of all animals, and one of the first to be domesticated. They are members of the cattle family and are related to sheep.

Goat hair is available in a loose mass of short staple hair. It also comes in roving. It is straight and bristly and a little coarser than camel hair. It can be spun alone or blended with wool and gives a highly textured surface when woven. It can be spun just like camel hair (see directions under camel hair).

Drawn goat hair is also available. This is sold in bundles of fibres drawn out so they lay parallel to each other. Drawn goat hair has a longer staple – from about six to 16 inches.

YAK

There are wild and domesticated yaks in Tibet and the adjacent highlands of central Asia. They are related to the ox, weigh about 1,200 pounds and measure five to six feet high at the shoulder. In Tibet they are used as beasts of burden and for their meat, milk, hide and hair. Wild yaks are black; however, the domesticated yaks vary in color. They can range from greyish and brownish to black. The back hair is short and smooth; on the rest of the body it grows in long waves reaching to the ground. The individual fibres are very strong, but are as smooth as straight black human hair.

Yak is available to handspinners in roving form. The staple is about six to eight inches long. Spin it the same as camel hair roving (see directions under camel). It is very bristly. Put on as much twist as possible without kinking. When spun with an even feed of fibres into the yarn you avoid overtwist in thin spots. Yak hair is not docile – ends of hairs will free themselves and will bristle out a few inches from the surface of the yarn. It is excellent for a coarse, highly textured yarn.

DOG AND CAT

Some of the best breeds for spinning are samoyed, husky and St. Bernard, which have an undercoat that can be brushed out. Longer staple, silky undercoats can be brushed from collies, sheep dogs and some hounds and retrievers. Poodles must be clipped rather than brushed, and this should be done after they have grown their maximum length coat. The hair of most other breeds is too short or slippery to spin alone, and many will shed even when blended with wool. Fur brushed from a Persian or angora cat can be spun, but the yield is small and it is not especially rewarding. With short-hair cats it is futile to try.

Try to get hair at least an inch long. It is easier to spin if the pet has not been bathed just prior to combing or clipping. Most fur needs no carding unless you blend it with wool. Throw away hairy or matted clumps that can't be just lightly teased and spun.

Follow the spinning directions for the kind of fibre most closely resembling that of the pet. Samoyed, husky and cat will be spun like angora rabbit. The wiry, bristly furs will mostly spin like camel hair or goat hair. After spinning, washing the fur with dog shampoo is excellent if you have it on hand. Dog fur often retains the dog's odor and these shampoos help deodorize it. Wash gently and put a dash of vinegar or lemon juice in the rinse water. If it is a light fibre, such as samoyed, weight the skeins lightly. Bristly furs with a tight twist, or furs blended with wool, can take a heavier weight.

PELT FURS

These include beaver, fox, wolf, muskrat, nutria, raccoon, etc. I do not use these fibres because it usually necessitates killing the animal. They live in the wild or are raised on farms for their pelts. Good pelts are used by furriers. Fur from rejected pelts and damaged pieces of pelt are usually blended with other fibres for commercially-made fabrics and sweaters.

If you insist on trying them, you will find them mostly fine, soft and slippery. Unless the staple is at least an inch long, you had better blend it with wool to make it cohesive and to produce a strong yarn. If it is well blended, it will give a soft hand to wool. If not well blended, it will slip and jerk while you spin. Yarn spun from such fur fibres will usually shed, even if tightly spun.

ANGORA RABBIT

Angora rabbits are members of the rodent family. They can live almost anywhere but are difficult to raise and don't yield much fibre – averaging only 12 ounces a year. The fur can be clipped or plucked. When clipped, the staple is one to three inches long. When brushed (plucked), it is two to four inches long. Different parts of the angora rabbit yield varying lengths and textures of the staple, but it is not practical to sort out unless you have an awful lot of rabbits. Angora fibre is extremely fine (average diameter 13 microns) and silky. It is available in white, shades of blue-grey, brown-grey and in black. It is sold by the pound or ounce, and since it is very light it goes a long way.

The fur must be loose and airy while being spun. It can be fluffed into a loose mass, or it can be gently carded. When you remove it from the carder, keep as many air spaces as possible. It is so light it can blow away without a breeze. Whether you are spinning a loose handful or a rolag, *do not clutch.* If damp or matted, it will not spin.

The fibres are short and slippery; loosely adjust the tension and treadle rapidly enough to put on a firm twist. After you have spun a yard, stop and test the yarn for strength, then adjust the tension again. Dip the skein and weight it lightly to set the twist – use a two to four-ounce weight. No matter how well it is spun, angora will always shed. It takes dye very well.

SILK

The origins of silk disappear into the wellsprings of myth and legend. It is possible the Chinese Empress Hsi-Ling-Chi really did accidentally drop a silk cocoon in her cup of tea. It is said that as she watched the filament unwind in the hot water, she realized it could be used as a fibre, and began to cultivate silkworms, and the white mulberry tree leaves on which they feed.

Silk was in use in China about 2,500 B.C., and by 1,500 B.C. the spinning and weaving of silk had been raised to a highly sophisticated level. In 125 B.C. the Silk Road was opened – a 6,000-mile caravan trek from China to the Mediterranean. Caravans returning to China took wool and Roman glass. After the Parthian Wars, traders brought beautifully woven silks to Imperial Rome – white silk as translucent as ice, gauze silk as light as a cloud, and colored brocades and embroideries.

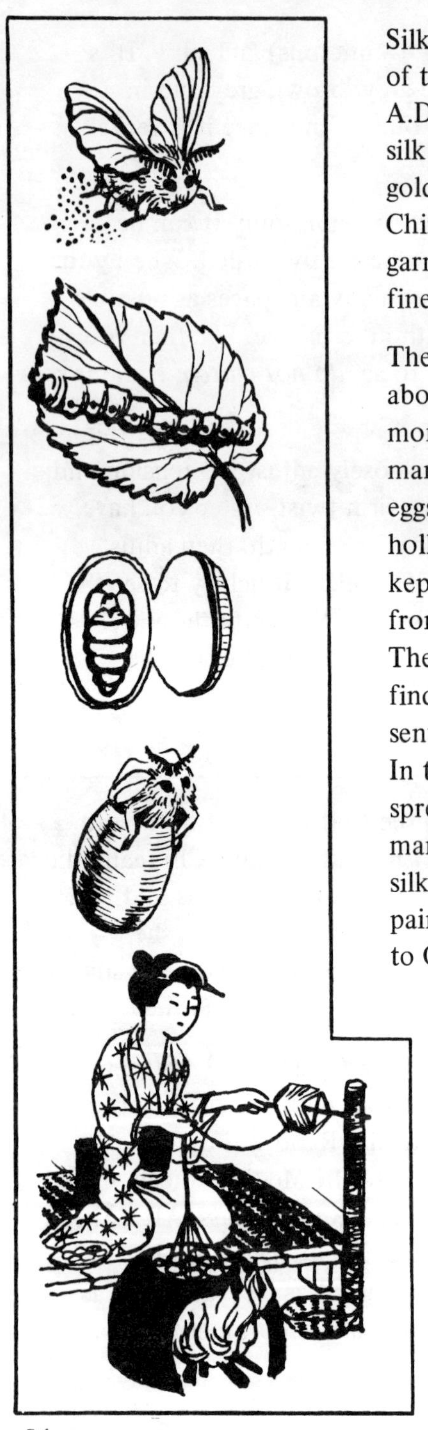

Silk became the most desired fabric of the Romans. In the third century A.D. it is recorded that a pound of silk in Rome was worth a pound of gold. A Roman scholar wrote, "The Chinese make precious woven garments bright like flowers and fine as a spider's web."

The silk industry began in the West about 552 A.D. Two Nestorian monks traveling through China managed to hide some silkworm eggs and mulberry leaves in a hollow cane – the Chinese had kept them a well-guarded secret from foreigners for 3,000 years. The two monks smuggled their find to Constantinople and presented it to the Emperor Justinian. In the next 500 years sericulture spread throughout Europe, and many major cities established silk industries. In 1598 the first pair of silk stockings was presented to Queen Elizabeth I of England.

Silk is the lightest and strongest fibre in the world. A silk filament is stronger than an equal size filament of steel, and stronger than any man-made fibre. It can hold 65,000 pounds per square inch. It has high elasticity and absorbency. Silk, like wool, insulates and does not readily conduct heat.

Thus, a silk garment is relatively warm in winter and cool in summer. When viewed under a microscope, silk filaments are smooth and translucent. Each cocoon is made of one continuous filament of this protein fibre. The egg of the silk moth (Bombyx-Mori) is about the size of a head of a pin. This hatches into a tiny worm that grows 10,000 times its original size in a month.

Cultivated silk worms feed on mulberry leaves and eat about 200 pounds of leaves to produce a pound of silk. Then they begin winding their cocoons, extruding the filament from glands on each side of their body, and cementing it in place with a soluble glue called sericin. After ten to twelve days, the silkworm transforms into a chrysalis, and then into a moth. It has a gland containing a drop of alkaline liquid which it spits out. This dissolves a hole in the cocoon large enough for the moth to escape, and the cycle repeats. Since the hole breaks the filament, most cultivated cocoons are not permitted to hatch before the filament is unwound.

This silk, when washed, is snowy white. Each cocoon yields one filament – about a half-mile long. The cocoons are soaked in hot water which dissolves the sericin, enabling the filaments to be reeled off. Filaments which are broken or damaged, and beginnings and ends of the cocoon, are processed in an uncombed mass and are sold as "silk waste". Or, they are combed into roving called "spun silk".

Silk tussah comes from the uncultivated silkworm, which feeds on the leaves of oak, castor and cherry trees. It is a golden color – varying from deep ivory to honey. Among handspinners, tussah is considered the most desirable kind of silk.

How to spin silk. You will find silk in many forms. For me the greatest joy is spinning silk tussah. This comes in a slim roving about a half-inch thick. It also comes in a brick-like package weighing about five ounces. Free the end that is tucked in and it will unwind in a long thick hank of roving. Loosen three or four filaments and fling them into the air – watch them float around the room before they slowly drift downward – lighter than a butterfly's wing. Take half a dozen filaments and twist them between your fingers and then try to break them. Notice how amazingly strong they are. Many people are so awed by the beauty of silk, they are afraid to spin it.

Pull off a piece about eight to ten inches long. It will be thick enough to divide lengthwise several times, making a more manageable piece of roving. Fold it over your forefinger (see diagram on page 17) and spin it exactly as you would any roving. You will find it draws very freely – provided the twist does not run up into the drawing-out triangle. If it should begin to overtwist, tighten the tension from the wheel, or else treadle more slowly. If it should drift apart, loosen the tension from your wheel, or speed up the treadling.

Quality of tussah varies. There is less expensive tussah which is available in roving. This is combed from a poorer quality waste. The staple is perhaps two to three inches. It has tiny tangles and bits of chrysalis and very little lustre. This will spin into an interesting, highly textured yarn. Spin it more slowly and with a looser tension.

Silk "waste" comes in many forms – sometimes in a cloudlike mass of short filaments. Pull a tuft of this loose and hold it up to the light. If the short filaments have many tiny knots and tangles, this is silk "waste" (damaged and broken filaments). You will be able to see the irregularities characteristic of this type.

Hold a cloud of it *loosely* in your hand. Don't clutch it. Damp, matted silk is harder to spin. Generally, you will spin it as you would a loose mass of wool. You will need slightly less tension from the wheel. Treadle a little more rapidly to give enough twist, since these filaments are sometimes short.

Silk also comes in semi-combed form and a handful of this looks like a shiny white rag mop. If you buy this you need only tease it, and can spin it as a glossy, highly textured yarn. To spin a finer yarn, card it with wool carders. But tease it first – because tangled silk is amazingly strong and can tear up the teeth of the carder. Put a small amount on the carder and brush lightly, like a fine wool. Fold it end to end in a pad. When I remove it from the carder, I like to fluff it up into an airy mass. This will give a nicely textured yarn – it is futile to try spinning silk uniformly smooth if it is not already in roving form.

Cocoons: If you insist on buying your own cocoons, try to get those from which the moth has already emerged (these will have a dark spot or hole at one end). Even those cocoons which produce white silk will look golden. Put them in a pot of hot soap suds and simmer for about a half hour. The gum will boil out, turning the water yellow. Drain in a colander and repeat the process. Rinse thoroughly and put it out to dry. It will look like a tangled white mass, When dry, pick out the bits of brown chrysalis. If you leave these bits in, you will have what the fashion industry sometimes calls "raw silk". To spin, follow the same directions as for semi-combed silk.

After spinning the silk and winding it off, and while it is still on the niddy-noddy, I lightly spray it with water. Then I twist it into a skein, put it in a plastic bag and set it in the refrigerator for a day. The moisture penetrates and sets the twist without in any way damaging the lustrous surface of the yarn. Silk will withstand heat up to 284° F. and sometimes industry will use heat to set the twist – but this won't work in a home oven.

To finish woven silk, I have found this method best: Don't dip it in water. Do lay it smoothly on your ironing board and set your steam iron for cotton. Hold the steaming iron an inch or two above the silk, moving it from side to side with the weft. Be careful not to touch the iron to the silk. Woven silk will shrink considerably – perhaps three inches for every 20 inches. Watch it move slowly inward. When thoroughly steamed it stops moving and reaches its maximum shrinkage.

COTTON

Archeological finds date the earliest known use of cotton to the Indus Valley 5,000 years ago. The earliest carbon dating for cotton in Peru is 2,500 B.C. At the same time, Egyptians were spinning and weaving cotton mummy cloth – at 540 ends per inch. India prints, much like those we now use, were being produced when the armies of Alexander marched into India. Phoenician traders carried cotton throughout the Mediterranean. The crusades, and the Arab conquest of Spain spread the use of cotton throughout Europe. One of the earliest reports of cotton to reach England was brought by Sir John Mandeville, returning from India in 1350. He wrote that "there grew there a wonderful tree which bore tiny lambs on the endes of its branches. These branches were so pliable that they bent down to allow the lambs to feed when they are hungrie." Shown is a woodcut from this medieval report. When Columbus landed in the New World, the Indians swam out to the ships with gifts – among them were balls of handspun cotton. In 1792, Eli Whitney invented the cotton gin for mechanically removing the seeds from the fibre – making possible large-scale production. Just one year before his invention, America shipped 400 bales of cotton to Europe. Within 20 years, the total was up to 180,000 bales a year.

Cotton is a seed fibre. The cotton grows as a protective covering around the seeds of the cotton plant, which reaches four to six feet high. When the cotton is picked it is about two-thirds seed, and only a third fibre. While growing, cotton is a single-cell tubular fibre. After being picked, it dries into a flat ribbon shape which twists or "corkscrews". This twist gives it the cohesiveness that allows it to spin easily. After being washed the cotton is about 98% cellulose. Like all vegetable fibres, cotton is 25 to 30% stronger when wet. It is highly absorbent, can be boiled safely and withstands heat up to 248° F.

Cotton is graded according to the quality of the fibre and the length of the staple. The length varies from three-quarters of an inch to two and a half inches. Quality is determined by the number of "corkscrews" per inch (the poorest has 150; Sea Island has 300). Sea Island, which originated off the coast of Georgia, is the highest quality – fine, silky, lustrous. Egyptian Sakel was cross-bred to produce Pima, which is very soft and lustrous. The bulk of the cotton grown in the U.S. is American Upland. Until 1965, consumption of cotton exceeded that of all other fibres combined – with jute running second.

Spinning cotton. Cotton has a reputation for being hard to spin. Don't believe it. Once you learn, it is a joy to spin, and can become positively addictive. It is inexpensive, so set aside a few ounces you don't plan to use for a project, and just use them for practice. After a little trial and error you will get the feel of it – and from then on it will become one of the easiest fibres to spin.

It is available in a fluffed mass that has had the seeds removed but that has not been combed. If you buy it in this form, it has been packed in compressed bales. Take a generous handful and fluff it up (see diagram on page 17). Put a very loose tension on your wheel. Remember, the staples are short and will need a lot of twist. Let the twist run up almost to your thumbnail. There should be just enough tug from the wheel so the twist can draw the fibres from the mass just under your thumb. Treadle rapidly as you move your right hand back somewhat slowly, in a long arm's length draw. Your left hand must not tug the fibres from your right hand. Use it just to guide, smooth and roll out lumps. Cotton in this form sometimes contains tiny flecks of seed hulls and produces a fine but textured yarn. When woven, it looks like a creamy, primitive African cloth or Mexican manta.

Cotton also comes in combed roving, usually a half-inch to one inch in diameter. It has no bits of seed in it and it naturally spins smoothly and more evenly. Do *not* double it over your finger. Do hold it just firmly enough so the tug of the wheel doesn't pull the whole roving through your hand. The twist will "eat" the fibres from the end of the roving. Don't forget to move your hand back as soon as the twist begins to catch – or the entire piece of roving will twist (see diagram on page 17).

Pima cotton in combed roving is also available. This will spin just like regular cotton roving, but is a little smoother, so it's better to learn on other kinds before you try Pima.

All cotton can absorb quite a lot of twist before it kinks. At first, put on as much twist as you can without having the yarn go into a corkscrew.

When you skein off your cotton, dip it in warm water and weight it with a half-pound weight for a four-ounce skein – enough to smooth out any kinks. After you spin several bobbins you will get an even twist without an overtwist. Then you can skip the skeining and dipping. Just set your wheel or lazy kate by your bobbin winder, and wind off directly from your spinning bobbin to your shuttle bobbins (quills).

When weaving cotton allow for plenty of shrinkage. Of course, this depends on the amount of twist in the yarn – but takeup and shrinkage in the weft can be as much as four to five inches in 36 inches.

KAPOK

Kapok is the silky fibre which protects the seeds of the tropical ceiba, or "silk cotton" tree. It is used for stuffing pillows, mattresses and life preservers. It is a beautiful golden beige and is very soft, but the staple is short and slippery. It is the only fibre that I have found I simply cannot spin.

COIR

This is a seed fibre and is taken from the outer husk of the coconut. It is used for brushes, doormats and cordage. The staple is six to eight inches, coarse, stiff and brittle. Occasionally it is used in wall hangings. It will spin more easily if you soak it in hot water overnight. Shake out the water and spin it while there is some dampness left in the fibre.

BAST FIBRES

Bast fibres are taken from the center stalk of a plant. They are long fibrous strands found between the outer bark and inner core of the stem. The seven widely used fibres in order of production are: jute, flax, hemp, sunn, ramie, kenaf and urena.

LINEN - FLAX

Linen and flax are the same. Flax is the name used for the plant and its fibre. Linen is the name for the spun yarn and woven fabric. Flax is the oldest fibre used by the human race. The earliest archeological find of plaited and woven construction dates it to 5,000 B.C. in the Valley of the Nile. It has been spun and woven for 7,000 years, so it obviously couldn't be as difficult to spin as some people say.

Egyptian wall paintings show the preparation of fibres and spinning. Phoenician traders spread the use of linen throughout the Mediterranean ports and it was introduced to the north by the Finns. It was our most commonly used textile fibre until the end

of the eighteenth century. Since linen grows so easily in many parts of the world, it never became an important article of trade. The colonists brought flax seed to America and established linen here. Linsey-woolsey – cloth woven with linen warp and wool weft – was widely used until the Civil War.

The stalk of the flax plant has a woody center surrounded by a ring of fibres and a layer of outer bark. The fibres are about 70% cellulose and have a high wax content, which gives linen its characteristic lustre. It is, with the exception of ramie, the strongest of all vegetable fibres. It can be boiled and has high heat resistance. It absorbs and evaporates moisture quickly, but has little elasticity and wrinkles easily.

You can grow flax in any temperate climate in about three months. There should be ample rainfall and sandy loam soil. Plant the seeds close together. When the plants mature, pull them up by the roots, dry in the sun and remove the seeds. Steep in a shallow, sunny pond, or any warm water, for one to two weeks until the outer bark decomposes. This is called retting. Then beat (scutch) it to separate the usable fibres. These fibres must then be combed (hackled) to clean and straighten them.

Spinning linen. Flax is not difficult to spin. When the long bundles of flax, with fibres up to three feet long, are combed, all the short pieces are combed out. These shorter pieces are called "tow". The very long remaining lengths are called "line". Probably the most common form of flax now available to handspinners is natural or bleached-white commercially-prepared roving. It has medium length staples – a mixture varying from three to four inches up to 15 or 18 inches. It is combed (hackled) and often is passed between hot, finely corrugated metal gears to give it a temporary crimp for easier spinning. If you buy it in this form, pull off a piece of roving eight to ten inches long, double it over your forefinger and spin, as shown in the diagram on page 17. This will give a rough, hairy-surfaced yarn.

A stronger, smoother yarn will result if it is wet-spun. Try this traditional way first: As your right hand is moving back, slide your left thumb over your wet tongue – then slide your left thumb and forefinger over the spun yarn – from the orifice back toward your right hand. See how all the hairiness disappears and leaves a smooth surface. Repeat this as you spin. If you want to be more hygienic, keep a bowl of water near the orifice of the wheel, and dip your left fingers in this.

If you have a mass of tow, you can spin it from the loose mass, or you can comb it. Tow is not as strong as line, but can produce a nicely textured weft.

Line has traditionally been spun from a distaff. The fibres are sometimes three feet long and so cannot be drawn out by the tug of the wheel or between your hands. Therefore your line has to be spun differently than other fibres. Try this simple method first:

Take your hank (strick) of line and lightly tie a cord near one end, just tightly enough so it will hang securely. Tie the ends of the cord in a loop and hang the hank high enough so the bottom end is two to three inches higher than the wheel orifice. Move your wheel to the spot where the hank is suspended about a foot from your right shoulder. You want to be able comfortably to pull the bottom fibres out of the hank with your right hand, and pass them toward the dampened thumb and forefinger of your left hand. You will constantly pull a few fibres *out* of the strick. This is one time you *do not draw your right hand backward* against the tug from the wheel. Generally, line should be spun finely – the wax content imparts a high lustre. And if you keep your thumb wet, it will be strong and smooth.

You will not need to dip linen to set the twist unless it was spun with an overtwist. If you do dip it, the skein will be stiff when it dries. Shake it a few times to soften. I have never seen woven linen shrink. It is best to wash it in a detergent or non-alkaline soap (don't use washing soda).

RAMIE

Ramie is often called China linen or China grass. It resembles a fine quality linen. It grows in southeast Asia, China, Japan and the Philippines. Now it is being cultivated in loam beds in the Everglades. Traditionally, degumming and separating the fibres was a long hand process. Recent technical advances have speeded up the process, and I hope it will again be on the market for handspinners.

Ramie is mainly used for paper, paper money, fire hose and filters. It is a white bast fibre with a very high lustre, and is highly resistant to heat and bacteria. It is the strongest of all vegetable fibres.

Spinning ramie. It is similar to linen but has a shorter, finer staple and is one of the easiest fibres to spin. It comes in roving. Spin it out from the end of the roving. Follow the diagram on page 17. The method is exactly the same as for cotton roving – except that you won't need as much twist on ramie as on cotton. And there won't be any shrinkage. For a smooth tightly spun yarn, you can wet-spin ramie (see linen). For an interesting, unusual yarn, blend ramie with clean raw mohair.

Ramie can be substituted in any project where you can use linen. Its translucence makes it ideal for curtains. When woven it appears like an exceptionally fine linen.

JUTE AND HEMP

Jute appeared in the Mediterranean and Asia in prehistoric times. Jute is used more than any other bast fibre. Most of our jute comes from India and Pakistan and is used mainly for burlap and twine. It has little elasticity and will rot when wet or damp for long periods. Jute is available in several shades of brown. Hemp probably originated in ancient China. It was the first fibre used for textiles in Japan. It is a grey-brown fibre, processed like flax, from the cannabis sativa. Russia is the world's largest producer. Remember, it is still illegal to grow your own. Jute and hemp feel scratchy, coarse and brittle. They are not particularly pleasant to spin. Both can be spun the same as linen. Some spinners use oil rather than water. I don't find this necessary. If you do use oil, be sure to wash it out thoroughly. Only if they are very overtwisted will jute and hemp need dipping in water.

LEAF FIBRES

Sisal and **hennequin** are fibres from the long-spike leaves of the agave plants. They are native to Mexico and were used by the pre-Columbian peoples. The agave will grow in desert areas with almost no rainfall, so its production has spread to other countries. Staples are 40 to 50 inches long, very strong and resistant to salt water. Handspinners can use sisal and hennequin for hangings and baskets. To spin them, soak overnight in hot water. Shake out the excess water and spin the same as line (see linen-flax section).

Abaca (manila hemp) is a three to nine-foot staple and is taken from the outer layer of the *musa textilis.* It is the best cordage fibre because of its strength and resistance to salt water (it is spun like sisal or line).

Ixtle, a leaf fibre from the *tula ixtle* of Mexico, is used for brushes, cordage and baskets.

Piña is derived from the spiky leaves of the pineapple plant. The fibres are very fine, silky and lustrous. Piña can be woven into a translucent, almost transparent cloth.

Raffia is a waxy fibre from the leaves of the raffia palm native to Madagascar. Varieties also grow in South Africa and South America. Soak it overnight and hang the damp hank as you would a hank of line (see linen). Feed the strips of raffia into the twist, one at a time, until you achieve the thickness you want. Just before you reach the end of each strip, begin twisting in another strip.

MAN-MADE FIBRES

Synthetic fibres are now available to handspinners in loose masses which need teasing or carding, and in roving – both white and dyed. You can spin them the same as wool, or blend them with wool. To set the twist, dip in quite hot water and let it drip-dry. If you squeeze the skein, it will wrinkle and not fluff up when dry. I find synthetics singularly unappealing in appearance and feel, and I do not use them because they are not a replenishable resource.

ANY QUESTIONS?

The availability of fibres, and the handspinning stores that supply them, change from time to time, so I have not included a list of sources. If you can't find a specific fibre – or have a special problem you can't solve – send me a stamped, self-addressed envelope and I will try to help you.